EXCLUSIVE FOR MEN

Things Women Find Unattractive in Men

Jefferson JOEL

EXCLUSIVE FOR MEN

(THINGS WOMEN FIND UNATTRACTIVE IN MEN)

Jefferson JOEL

CONTENTS

- **Irresponsibility**

CHAPTER THREE

APPEARANCE

- **Unsanitary (personal hygiene)**

- **Bad breath**

- **Cologne overload**

- **Random hair (unkempt hair)**

- **Bad manners**

- **Tan sunscreen**

- **Excessive tattoos**

- **Dirty fingernails**

- **Wearing ill-fitting incompatible dress**

CHAPTER FOUR

- **Conclusion**

INTRODUCTION

The unattractive feeling is terrible. It can be difficult to know if it's all in your head. And sometimes all you have to do is recognize the signs that you are unattractive and deal with them. Correct it and no matter how you look or feel now, you will soon be your own sexiest version.

Some of the highest rated "characteristics" that women find unattractive in men fall under arrogance, lack of chivalry, boasting, video gaming, lying and being irresponsible. So keep those in mind -- but as far as just physical appearance is concerned, avoid unnecessary mistakes that will scare women away from you and imbibe strategies that increase your attractiveness exponentially.

CHAPTER ONE

Things women find unattractive in men

Things women find unattractive in men can be categorized into two;

1. Character
2. Physical appearance

Character: Mental and moral qualities worthy of a person.

Great characters are always more attractive than those with great faces, but not everyone likes to carve out places in their hearts. In this way, beauty attracts attention, but characters are captivating!

Physical Appearance:

Appearance defines the characteristics and features of the human body. These are aspects of a person's appearance that others can see without further information about that person. They can contain many different things. Hair and facial features play a big role, but not all.

Physical features are visible to the naked eye. They cover all the ways in which the physical characteristics of an individual or group of people can be explained based on what is observable to the eye.

CHAPTER TWO

CHARACTER:

Some ugly features that accompany Character includes;

Pride:

Pride, or the act of being proud, is usually accustomed to describe a way of deep satisfaction toward yourself or somebody near to you.

As a temperament attribute, pride will fight a unique meaning.

While it's still related to a way of complacence, pride may also be a manifestation of a desire for dominance or status, and problem of accepting one is also wrong.

These tendencies may come out in various behaviors, such as:

- Refuse to compromise or find difficulty in accepting challenges.

- Always angry with the other person's opinion.

- Always find the flaws of others when comparing to yourself.

- Judge some tasks under your dignity and refuse to do them.

- Refuse to apologize, even if you realize you can resolve the dispute.

- The feeling of always knowing what's best and what's wrong with the other person.

Arrogance

- Ignoring the opinions of others. You may feel reassured about your decisions and thoughts, but not giving the thoughts of others may be arrogant. "An arrogant person doesn't value a different opinion, and if he disagrees, he considers it a contempt or an attack." It's your achievement, but you also recognize the role of others.

- You don't appreciate others "Give credit whenever you need credit, as the achievements of others do not hurt your achievements.

- You are talking about others:. " Arrogant people interfere with conversion and dominate often, the need to talk about others can result from the need to feel what you have heard and find a test of your thoughts. To gain their trust, you need to listen.

- You place your relationship above others: But arrogance makes meaningful partnerships difficult. This is because this egocentrism is often associated with the need to downplay people.

- You don't accept feedback

" Arrogant men find it difficult to accept feedback and take an attitude on my road or highway." If you find yourself in this category, Take a step back and reassess your response to feedback. After all, the people who provide feedback often have your greatest concern in mind, so take a light comment. Women feel safe to be with men who accept feedback.

- You worry about what people think about you: Confident people do not need constant verification from others. "Confidence means being warm and kind to others without being overly worried about how you will be received ... and telling others how wonderful they are.

- Feels frustrated when things don't go your own way.

"Arrogance is based on fear because it's based on anxiety and reliance on external verification, which helps with more difficult emotions such as fear, frustration, and anger."When life isn't going as the arrogant people want, there feelings become apparent and tend to blame others on the situation rather than seeing the role they played in the situation." And give a sense of belonging.

Lack of chivalry (Courtesy)

- It is interpreted simply as meaning the courtesy of men to women. For some, chivalry embraces the most desirable qualities women seek from men. No matter who she is or what background she came from, every woman wants a charming prince.

Who is the girl who doesn't enjoy being taken to dinner? A man who buys flowers and chocolates, a man who opens car doors, a man who opens all doors, a man who takes a long walk, a man who takes a clock, who doesn't care about sunset? Most girls dream of this knight's jewel. WOMEN CHERRIES CHIVALRY!

Lies

The word "lie" quickly creates a vision and a terrible negative sensation. It embodies the morals that most people want to avoid.

- Lies destroy trust: Perhaps the most obvious effect a lie has on relationships is the loss of trust that one person has with the other. Lies and trust cannot simply coexist. Eventually the former destroys the latter.

- Lies show a lack of respect: When told the truth, whatever it is, the recipient feels respected. It proves to them that you put great value on the relationship and are willing to trick them into putting them at risk.

- Waiting for the liar to slip again: After you lied for the first time, it's hard not to live in anticipation of the future truth from you. They start wondering what you're saying and shed your words on the internal alert system for signs of fraud.

- Lies show selfishness: When you lie, you essentially prioritize your own interests over theirs. Not wanting to make a sacrifice for the greater, long-term benefits of a relationship is another indicator that you are not evaluating it. Lies are also a sign of widespread selfishness, ignoring others, which can make them feel unloved and undesired.

- They find it stupid to believe a lie: The moment they realize you lied is the most unpleasant. When their eyes are truly open, they cannot help feeling stupid about falling to lies.

When you make them feel this way, all the positive feelings you have towards them are consumed. Pain can open gaps between you, or it can simply cause old cracks to resurface and spread.

- Lies upset the balance of relationships: In order for your relationship to withstand the challenges of time and survive the challenges of everyday life, both parties must devote equal commitment and energy to it. This balance creates a sense of partnership that allows you to stick together and bring out the best of each other.

- Lying can upset this natural balance and cause the scale to tilt. To those who lie, they can feel like they are in line with their hearts and souls just to keep you in check.

- Lies tell lies: It's not uncommon for one lie to lead to another and a futile attempt to deceive someone into another. You may even be a habitual liar who sees nothing wrong with talking to a woman in the piggy bank of your life.

When lies become commonplace, relationships are harmed and cannot survive. Women hate lies!

Irresponsible

- Fearing responsibilities: commitment perhaps he simply does not wish to commit to something specifically. Having him hang around with you is like coitus interruptus his teeth.

- He doesn't settle for mistakes: Instead, he points his finger at everybody. He's not the sort to require responsibility forthwith. And if you manage him, he can continually know how to shake off the blame.

- You do not have a regular job: this guy could never be a regular worker. Instead, you will notice that he's continually vital to his work. She could feel that you just lack ambition and you solely speak heaps concerning yourself.

- There was no significant relationship: Once discussing past relationships, you never mention long-run relationships. Instead, speak solely concerning one night's stand or one month's stand.

- You're terribly vulnerable. you frequently cave in during a blink of an eye fixed. It's okay to be upset from time to time, however overdoing it during a relationship will cause issues.

- You're indecisive. "She continually felt that she was creating choices not just for the expansion of the connection, however additionally for you. you permit most of the decisions to her, that is usually quite frustrating."

- You are very uncaring: you may sometimes be very selfish. Your priorities are very different and "more important". She may be upset when she realizes that you are thinking only about yourself and not others.

- No real life plans, you don't know what you want to do professionally. You live your daily life and prefer to take it when things come. Women hate future unambiguous men!

CHAPTER THREE

APPEARANCE:

These set of behaviors turn women off from being close to men.

1. Unsanitary (Personal hygiene)

This is the number one turn-off for all women. She understands that you smell like BO after a basketball game, but you shouldn't smell that when you pick her up for dinner or just hang out. There are all kinds of deodorants. Find something that works for you and take a shower regularly. Women love the cleanliness and the "fresh" scent from the shower.

2. Bad breath

If your breath is fainting her, she will want to keep herself away-preferably away from some states. Get a tongue scraper (yes, they have them, and yes, they make a big difference!), Brush and rinse your mouth several times a day, gum or breath as needed. Keep the mint handy.

3 Cologne Overlord (Scent)
Don't get me wrong, women love good scents. Especially when it comes from our guy. But when you are dressed enough to walk in the clouds of Cologne, we really can't breathe. It is important to maintain a good midpoint. It smells good, but don't overbear it.

4. Random Hair (unkempt hair)
We're not just talking about greasy scalp hair. Also talk about excessive hair (ears, nose, etc.). And if your back and chest get out of control, do something about it. That

is, we shave our feet for you several times a week.

5. Bad manners

Burp and toilet humor has time and place. Sometimes It slip, but doing so always makes her feel like she is in a room with a lot of 5-year-old boys.

6. Tan Sunscreen

This may seem strange, but it is true. Females do not like the appearance of male raccoons. Use a small sunscreen-reduces the risk of skin cancer and keeps the skin color uniform.

7. Excessive tattoos

Many women love the look of clean skin and can sometimes distract from full-body tattoos. If you really want it, don't hide it.

8. Dirty fingernails
She holds your hand and you touch her face with them. So keep your nails short and clean.

9.You wear an ill-fitting, incompatible dress (improperly dressed).
Blurred, baggy clothes are as fashion fake as the wrong women's little mini dresses. Find the one that suits you and the one that corresponds to your age!
Throw away your old sweatpants and go buy a brand new wardrobe! If you don't know what kind of clothes to wear, go to a department store and help your personal

shopper give you advice and choose the right clothes for you.

CHAPTER FOUR

Conclusion

Taking time to take care of yourself will increase your self-confidence, make you feel better, and people will love being with you. A well-maintained look tells you all kinds of good things. And yes, this is all very attractive to women.

Remember that being attractive is a combination of inner and outer beauty. Take care of your appearance and try to stay healthy and fit, but don't forget that it's also good to be nice. Otherwise, no matter how beautiful you are, people will not be able to see it.